INVENTING
SMALL PRODUCTS
for Big Profits, Quickly

INVENTING SMALL PRODUCTS

for Big Profits, Quickly

STANLEY I. MASON

CRISP PUBLICATIONS

Editor-in-Chief: *William F. Christopher*

Managing Editor: *Kathleen Barcos*

Editor: *Janis Paris*

Cover Design: *Kathleen Barcos*

Cover Production: *Russell Leong Design*

Book Design & Production: *London Road Design*

Printer: *Bawden Printing*

Library of Congress Card Catalog Number 97-65792

ISBN 1-56052-436-7

CONTENTS

PART I
LEARNING TO BECOME AN INVENTOR   1

I.   FIRST LESSONS IN INVENTING   3

II. LEARNING TO LEARN   7
     Learning to be a Good Student   9

III. HOW TO BECOME A PROFESSIONAL INVENTOR   15
     Searching for Needs   15
     The Invention Process   16
     Presenting the Product   22

PART II
EXAMPLES OF SUCCESSFUL INVENTING   25

IV. INVENTIONS THAT CHANGE
     AND IMPROVE EXISTING PRODUCTS   27
     How to Invent a Product Using Other People's Skills   27
     Always Say, "Yes, I Can Do It"   30
     How Can an Inventor Market a New Product?   31
     Making a Product Better by Asking the Users   36
     How Do You Change and Improve a Product?   37

V.   INVENTIONS OF NEW PRODUCTS   43
     How to Learn about a New Product Area   43
     Experimentation–Inventing New Products for
        New Technology   44
     How Do You Make an Old Product New?   48
     How to Develop a New Product and Sell It   52

CONTENTS

How to Invent a Product to Fill a Need   54
Sometimes a Problem Will Help Create a Product   56
Inventions Can Be New Methods   57
Taking Risks: The Difference between
      Consultants and Employees   59

PART III
SOME OF THE FUNDAMENTALS   **63**

VI.   ADDITIONAL THOUGHTS
      THAT MAY BE HELPFUL TO YOU   65
        Meeting Your Prospect   70

VII. LAST THOUGHTS   77

APPENDIX: CREATIVITY   81

FURTHER READING   91

ABOUT THE AUTHOR   93

PART I

LEARNING TO BECOME AN INVENTOR

I.

FIRST LESSONS IN INVENTING

I'M AN INVENTOR OF ordinary, everyday products—not high-tech, but common useful things. Who starts off wanting to invent such products? Virtually nobody. Inventors, in general, work on the big-time kinds of ideas which interest them. But there is big opportunity in inventing small and useful products. This book describes how to do it.

What sort of invention was my first? I truly was not trying to make an invention, but to satisfy my own personal need for 15 cents. I had asked my father, when I was seven years old, for 15 cents to buy minnows to go fishing in the broad canal behind our property in Trenton, New Jersey. He turned me down. He said that fishing was not an admirable use of time and, therefore, he kept his darned 15 cents.

My mother was a creative observer of that conversation, and she asked me why didn't I make an artificial minnow that would last a long time. She gave me a wooden clothespin to use. I looked at the clothespin and realized it was fairly close to the size of a minnow and, with a little whittling with a paring knife, I was able to make it roughly into the shape of a minnow. I added a hook at one end and an eye at the other, and was so enthusiastic about my creation that I immediately went fishing. As I cast it into the canal, I realized that it would absorb water, and though it attracted fish, they did not bite; they simply came over and looked at it, and all I saw was the whirl of water where their fins had churned. I went back into my father's shop in the basement and whittled out another minnow while my first one dried.

I went into the encyclopedia and looked at the kinds of colors I should paint on the side of my minnow. They weren't very fancy—green, black and white. I roughly duplicated the photo and it was quite a credible minnow.

I took it out into the canal and tied it onto my line and gave it a trial. It was quite spectacular, and within twenty minutes I caught a beautiful bass!

I generated all kinds of interest with my minnow, and soon I was in business selling minnows. Ten neighborhood kids went home and borrowed 25 cents for their minnow. Business was much more gratifying than fishing, because every 15 minutes I was able to earn a quarter.

I really had learned a great lesson: first of all I had created a product that people wanted. Second, it was a demonstrable product. Third, my market (though small) was very anxious to have the product. Fourthly, it was possible to modify my first design with different colors and shapes, so I had a product line quite quickly.

I continued my minnow business until I learned that I could easily build and sell boomerangs. It was 1928, the year Lindberg flew across the ocean, and I was enamored with all kinds of gliders, airplanes and birds.

My boomerangs were simply L-shaped wings made of plywood, and I could make many, many by sawing out one L-shape right next to the other, from one 4′ × 8′ piece of plywood. I would then sandpaper air foil sections on the front and rear of each of the wings.

They would fly beautifully, each one somewhat differently, but most would return if thrown the right way. I could get $1.00 for each boomerang, yet it only cost me

Figure 1. The Mason minnow business

12 cents to make. I soon learned that I could hire my friends to saw out the pieces and other friends to sand them. This was a great learning experience because it was possible to make much money by simply drawing the lines.

II.

LEARNING TO LEARN

THE MOST IMPORTANT FAMILY impression for me was my mother who saw to it that at age eight I began art school.

I walked down to the center of town, and every Saturday for five years, went to a class in free hand art. My first teacher, Mr. Schulman, believed implicitly that every student should learn observation. He came to the first class late, passed out a paper, pulled down the window shades, and asked the students to draw what was outside of the windows. The classroom was square with glass windows all the way around and overlooked the city.

Hardly any of the students knew what was outside of the window, and only drew what they imagined might be out there. At the second session, all the students carefully looked out of the windows, but were asked to draw a shadow box in the corner of the room which Mr. Schulman had covered up with a cloth. We had to draw what was in the shadow box. Time after time, we were asked to draw things which were common, such as knives and forks, and the front of our houses, etc. Gradually we became obsessed with being aware of our environment.

This is the sort of background which is necessary for a successful inventor, to know where she or he is at all times and to be able to draw a picture of it to show an understanding of what the view is.

The series of classes in the art school began with a year of pencil, then a year of pen and ink, then a year of watercolor, a year of oil painting landscapes and then a year of drawing people. Each of these classes had professional artists teaching. This kind of background is very useful to inventors.

My father was a great help in setting up my businesses. I used his shop in the basement, loaded with all

Figure 2.   Learning to draw

kinds of equipment and tools such as a drillpress, power saw, lathe and vise. We also had a foundry where I could make hundreds of soldiers from a mold that I had purchased from a hobby shop.

Because my father had a shop, I always knew how to make things, and I never underestimated the value of this knowledge. My father explained how the tools worked, and how the machines were dangerous. And he allowed me to use them as long as I cleaned up the shop when finished.

Learning to be a Good Student

School was always a special problem with me because it always seemed to me that school was in my way. When I went to school in the morning, I hated to go because it took me away from the shop. School really did not help my progress. It kept me from doing the kinds of things which I had planned to do at home. There were many schooltime activities I thought were boring, but the one thing that really started me on the wrong foot was the fact that before I went to kindergarten my uncle had already taught me to read. So, my teacher didn't like me very much because what could she teach?

My mother followed me to school many days with a switch, making sure that I got there. During the two-block walk, I would often find something of great interest along the way . . . something much more interesting than going to school.

In the third grade the principal locked me in her office because I would not color within the lines of the class book. I figured I had much more interesting kinds of art to create. While in her office I determined that her method of organizing her files was incorrect. The filing cabinets were arranged alphabetically–A, B, C–in the first cabinet, then up to the second cabinet D, E, F. It occurred to me that if the files were arranged horizontally, papers would be easier to file and to locate. So, I spent the day reorganizing her filing according to my method. No one ever said anything about this, and when I left the school the files were still organized horizontally, rather than vertically.

When my mother took my brother, nine years younger, to register at the Peabody School, the same principal met my brother and said to my mother, "I hope he's not as bad as the first one." My mother marched out of her office and registered my brother at another school.

My report cards until I was in the ninth grade were so terrible that my daughter later hid them from my grandchildren. The teachers always talked about my daydreaming and my lack of attention to assignments. Then in the ninth grade I had a math teacher who understood the kind of tasks that interested me. Suddenly, all of my grades became honor grades. This was true throughout high school.

I always had projects to build in the shop, and I had great enthusiasm for everything I did. I always had more than enough to do and was never bored. I always had money because I was always making things, shoveling snow or cutting the lawns of neighbors. I designed and built small doll houses, which I painted and sold. I also built and sold model yachts to sail in the canal.

One day I went to the Trenton Public Library, a white marble building, very stately and large. I talked to the librarian, and she hired me to be a page. My contract was to work in the library from 4:00 p.m. until 9:00 p.m., and I was paid 25 cents an hour to reshelve books.

I worked in the circulation department, which had all the fiction and nonfiction books. The technical department was on the third floor, and the reference room on the second floor. I was often sent to these rooms for books. It was an exciting time, and every day I learned something different.

I was the kid who eventually learned all the authors, all the fine books—fiction and nonfiction. I moved from the circulation department and spent a year with the children's department, a subsequent year with the reference room and, later, the technology department. I truly learned more in the library than I ever learned in high school.

The library was an impressive and important part of my background for inventing because I learned very quickly that everything had a number. There were always so many of this and so few of that, and everything had a name, and if you knew how many and the name of the subject, you could categorize and learn lots of subject matter. Because of my work at the library, school was always extremely easy, and I very seldom did any homework because I learned enough in class to get good grades on examinations.

I became an enthusiastic student in high school and was editor of the high school newspaper where I learned to write news and feature stories. I never really had a standard English course, because as editor of the newspaper,

I was excused from English classes. My teachers always wanted me to be in the student government, but that would have gotten in the way of working at the library.

Each morning at 4:30 a.m., I would race out of bed, eat my breakfast, and ride my bike one block to where they deposited my stack of newspapers. This was my real entrepreneurial training, because I was delivering the newspaper in one of the most prestigious, wealthy neighborhoods. I learned that rich people don't pay their bills, and it took special kinds of tasks to get them to pay. The 14 cents a week was a task for them. I trained most of my customers to leave the money in the vestibules. I liked the coolness of the large mansions and the clean smell of the maids. My goal, of course, was to do such a good job of serving the newspaper route that I would receive not only the pay for the newspaper, but large Christmas gifts—in some cases up to $5.00.

It was always my impression that if people didn't get good grades, it was because they didn't try, not because they weren't bright. I've learned since that intelligence is everything, and some people are smarter than others. Inventors need to work with smart people.

Two weeks before graduation from high school, my mechanical drawing teacher came to my desk and sat next to me. "What are you going to do when you graduate?" he asked. I said I hadn't really thought about it because I thought I would work with my father. My father had his own business of doing electrical work for all kinds of companies and private individuals in their homes. He could use my help. My teacher asked me if I had thought about college. I replied I hadn't. I did have a cousin who went to Princeton, and I thought that was a nice idea—but his father paid for Princeton, and my dad would not pay for anything. My teacher then asked why didn't I go to State College in Trenton? He told my they were having an examination for a scholarship the next day. I went to the examination, which was six hours long, and it really was easy. They corrected the exams, and I won the scholarship and went to college. The strange thing was that the school was 10 miles away, but it never occurred to me that it might be a problem getting to school, working in the library and delivering my newspapers. I didn't worry because everything can always be worked out. It's one foot in front of the other.

Because of my examination grades, I was able to take all the classes that my time would allow. I even got credit for some of the courses I took the examination for. I was an Industrial Arts major, but also a Science major, and an English major. It was all very easy. I listened very carefully in every class and seldom needed to do any homework.

I was in a special category because I lived at home, while most of the students lived in the campus dormitories. I really didn't get to know other students very much at all and truly didn't care. It was like a continuation of high school.

III.

How to Become a
Professional Inventor

A S A CREATIVE PERSON, you must look at yourself as a special kind of person, one who can invent in a wide spectrum of fields. Your "specialness" is not limited to one invention, in one field, unless you are an employee of a company hired to work in one area.

As an independent inventor, you have the world to invent in, but you need to, I believe, carefully choose your fields.

Searching for Needs

I believe it's important to carefully review the need for an invention and then to select a company that already has production facilities as well as a market presence in that category of need.

In other words, you may spend as much time looking for the proper area in which to invent as you might in the development of the invention. You should be sure to invent in a product area where there is a need, and not invent first and then seek a purchaser of your invention.

There are many ways to find product needs. One good way is to become very familiar with your local hardware store, your local supermarket and your local drug store. Visit these stores at least weekly until you understand all the categories of products for sale.

Soon you will begin to know the personnel in the store, perhaps by name, and they will begin to tell you when new products are being put on their shelves. Gradually you'll learn the "hot" categories, and you will begin to think of small or large improvements in the new products placed on the shelves. You will gradually build an awareness of a broad range of product categories and the small improvements that gain sales in the stores that you have selected as your models of review.

In talking with beginning inventors who have working models of their concepts, I am frequently asked, "How do I sell my invention?" It's important I believe, to establish a list of potential buyers of an invention before the details of that invention are puzzled out. It's a serious problem when an inventor spends all of his or her time creating an invention for which he or she hasn't the slightest idea of who may buy it.

I believe that a successful inventor is one who senses a need for a product, determines what sort of strategy to pursue to sell the invention, and then launches into a program of development of that invention.

The Invention Process

For the last forty years, I have personally followed a careful process for the development of products. Figure 4

Figure 3. Observe and learn

indicates how I organize my thinking and my time, and the time of various scientists who can help me develop products outside of my own expertise.

Phase I—Search & Appraisal

The first thing I do is form my task into a single sentence with the words, "How do I develop a _____? (This sentence should include the goal of my product or invention.) Therefore, if I'm developing an insecticide or a new cookie, or a new bandage, everyone on the team that

Phase I
Search & Appraisal
Don't try to invent; just learn.
Write a product definition and specifications.
Search out existing similar products.

Phase II
Product System Concept
Make careful drawings of "How it might be."
Make many, many sketches and drawings.

Phase III
Prototype Development
Select best directions and develop "How you do it."
Produce a working model.

Phase IV
Precommercialization
Establish what kind of machine will make the product.
Detail the costing.

Figure 4.   Four stages of product development

I have created knows specifically what our goal is, and does not wander off on peripheral (but great) ideas.

I then decide, "When do I want to have this invention or product developed?" I know I can't do it in one day, and I know that it must be done in less than a year, so I estimate the complexity of the undertaking.

I divide my thinking patterns into four categories. The first category is "Search & Appraisal." If it's a small product, I can estimate that my Search & Appraisal effort will take under six months but over one month, and so I estimate perhaps three months.

I then select several assistants or helpers to research what is known in the world about the product category that I'm planning to invade.

My first source is the patent office, and I study the category within which the product will fall. I ask my patent attorney for help. I think very seriously about the subject, visiting all kinds of stores, all kinds of places where similar products are in use.

I'll hold meetings with four to six people in a group and learn what divergent ideas they may have of the category. I don't expect them to invent, just to tell me what exists. I'll keep careful notes and develop a scrapbook which has ads, catalog pages and descriptions of existing products or concepts.

Phase II—Product System Concept

When I have exhausted all possible directions, the Second Phase becomes the Concept Phase. During this phase, I take an indelible pencil and develop all kinds of sketches, drawings and photographs of existing products with my unique idea incorporated into them. Perhaps 100 or 200 detailed felt tip sketches are developed.

I hold frequent meetings with various people who are also sketching new ideas, aiming to satisfy the question, "How do I develop a ⎯⎯⎯⎯⎯⎯⎯⎯⎯?" The 200 sketches are carefully analyzed, compared one with the other, with all kinds of questions in mind: How much will it cost to make the product? How fast can it be manufactured? What kinds of materials will be used? How much power will it require? What is the process of manufacturing? Who is an expert in this field? Will it be injection molded? . . . all kinds of questions regarding how to make the product.

Focus groups are held showing various sketches to get the reaction of the potential users of the product. All people who are part of a Focus Group or an important team sign a Confidentiality Agreement with me so that I can maintain the secrecy of the product.

Phase III—Prototype Development

When all of the possible sketches that I or my assistants have conceived are completed, we move to the next phase, which is Development. In the Development Phase we convert a small number of the best concepts in drawing form into a three-dimensional, full-scale functioning model. We try very hard to keep the development of models at the lowest possible cost. If, for example, the finished product would be injection molded, we would perhaps make the model from clay and fire it so we get a sense of how it's going to look and feel and how practical it will be. We use lots of alternative materials in our model development. We may carve the new plastic bottle out of wood so that we have a sense of space. We paint the model to replicate competitive products that we find in the market. We buy competitive products and place them on a store shelf in our studio so that we can put the model of the new product in its proper environment on a store shelf. If we're developing shoe polish, it would be among competitive shoe polish, for example.

We then try very hard to visit the manufacturer and/or marketer of existing products which are for sale in the stores. Before we would show our product to those manufacturers/marketers, we would attempt to gain a Confidentiality Statement from that company. Ideally, we would visit three or four competitors in the field.

We've found that the company who is #1 in the field is usually least interested in talking with us, whereas the #2 or 3 will usually sign a Confidentiality Statement. Failing this, we will develop a patent statement for our patent attorney to work with, and he will attempt to gain a patent for us.

Phase IV—Precommercialization

By this time, we will have a relationship with several of the manufacturers and will have established a certain amount of interest in seeing our new product. We will not have told them anything except some of the characteristics of our new product, with particular emphasis on the fact that our new invention makes obsolete some of the major characteristics of the product they are currently selling in the stores.

It's important that we do know the costs of the product that we've developed, the production techniques, the amount of tooling, the cost of the tooling, the production rates, the estimated wholesale and retail selling price and an estimate of the volume of sales which are expected. We will have sponsored marketing research of our product vs. the existing product to determine whether or not there is a true want and need in the market of our new and improved product.

When you do all the development work outlined above, you will have carefully determined your product's estimated cost of manufacture so you know whether it's a reasonable price for the manufacturer/marketer as well as a reasonable retail price for the consumer. In general, the cost of manufacturing will be doubled for the wholesale price, and the wholesale price will be doubled for the retail price. This is known as the Keystone method of costing; that is, the price that the consumer will pay is four times the cost to manufacture the product. Such a number includes all kinds of costs—advertising, commissions, royalties, etc. It's a good rule of thumb.

A product which you find in direct mail catalogs will have a similar ratio of price to cost. In general, the price that you find in such catalogs is about five times the actual cost of manufacture. Direct Mail or Direct Response catalogs are the result of a complex system of testing. An inventor should not count on selling a product through catalogs without first discussing with the catalog marketing department whether or not they would run a product to be invented through this complex statistical system of evaluation prior to placing it in the catalog.

Presenting the Product

It is important for you, the inventor, to know how to make a presentation very efficiently and effectively.

You need to present your product to the audience in an efficient and entertaining way. You shouldn't worry about whether prospects are interested in the technical details, but only that they can make money with the invention and want to buy or license the patent. Don't get anxious—all you really need to do is to interest prospects to the point where they will take the initiative and ask,

"How much?" When they do that, you have a genuine buying signal that there is great interest. Be sure you have the answer ready, and then tell them what the best way to purchase is.

I have often been asked about invention marketing companies. In my experience you, the inventor, will be more effective in marketing your invention using the ideas and methods described in this book.

Lastly, join your local inventors group. Other inventors will help you solve the problem of how to make your prototype and, perhaps, how to sell it.

Be honest in your dealings and forthright.

Figure 5.   *Presenting the product*

PART II

EXAMPLES OF SUCCESSFUL INVENTING

IV.

INVENTIONS THAT CHANGE AND IMPROVE EXISTING PRODUCTS

THE FOLLOWING EXAMPLES OF successful inventions describe methods inventors use:

- To identify and appraise needed changes and improvements in an existing product

- To invent/develop a product that will better satisfy customer needs

- To successfully market the invention

There are many roads to success, but the right road for any inventor begins with finding an opportunity and setting a goal.

How to Invent a Product Using Other People's Skills

How does invention take place?

The head of research of a large potato chip company, for whom we had worked for 12 years, was suddenly terminated. They had a new Senior Vice President appointed who did not need the kind of talent my friend possessed.

I helped the former researcher create his resume and soon he had a new job as vice president of a minority-owned company in the cosmetic business. (Keep close track of friends and your network.)

This friend called me and, with great surprise, said he had just learned that one of their products, a hair straightening agent, used lye as a straightening chemical which, of course, was very dangerous, and could easily harm the eyes of users.

I visited with him and he asked if I thought I could create a hair straightening chemical which would have a pH of 5 and, therefore, be very safe to use around the eyes.

I was not a chemist, but I thought it could feasibly be done. (Anything can be done.) I accepted the assignment and laid out a proposal which the board agreed to. I said that in one year I would create a chemical which would be safe, acceptable and pleasant to use, and would straighten the hair of black customers. I went back to my office and thought about how would I go about finding the kind of people who could develop this product. I placed classified ads in the local newspaper: "Wanted, Ph.D. level chemist with experience in permanent waving of hair. A phone number was listed.

We received 50 resumes. I reviewed them and called in and hired three people. One was a young Ph.D. who had just been fired by a hair care company. The second was the head of a cosmetic company laboratory who had just retired and was setting up his own company. The third was an elderly professor of chemistry from a local college who had heard every question freshmen can ask.

I interviewed these three separately, and gave them the assignment of thinking about "How would you develop a hair care product that would permanently wave hair, something that would use natural products."

I suggested an analogy of thinking about meat tenderizer (meat is a protein and so is hair). I told them to think about the Venus Fly Trap which is a plant that catches flies and eats them with its own chemistry. I asked them to think about other analogies that would use natural products.

I did not tell them that there were three people working on the project. I talked as though each was the only one involved. I asked each one to think about the subject for a week and come back and report. When the first person came in, I took careful notes of his thoughts. When the second came, I took notes and told him what the first man had told me. When the third person came, I took careful notes and told him what the first two people had told me.

This routine went on for ten weeks, with experiments in their homes and reporting in my office. In this way we were able to build a technique of discovery in an area that I didn't understand initially. In ten weeks, we had directions which could be explored experimentally and tested on the hair of black women.

We made many samples of the product, with minor modifications, and tested them on 100 women's hair in three different beauty salons catering to black women.

We gradually improved the product again and again, until we made our major presentation to the client. The product was highly successful. All in all, it was a very successful program with the product made on schedule and within budget.

This description outlines how it's possible to develop a product successfully, but outside of one's own personal skills.

Always Say, "Yes, I Can Do It"

Inventors know almost every problem is solvable. The day after I set up Simco in the space above my garage, I was telephoned by the VP of Research and Development of one of the big pharmaceutical companies. He said, "Could you come down to my office and speak with me?" Naturally, I said yes.

He described that they needed to make a placenta basin, a basin used to catch the placenta in childbirth, that would not attract electricity, that would be anti-stat. I asked him all the proper questions—"What is a placenta basin?" "How does it work?" "Why should it be anti-stat?"

He explained, the doctor leans against the table with a small basin, 6″ by 6″ by 4″, with the patient on the far side, and he scoops out the placenta into the basin. The placenta is sold by the hospital to manufacturers who make gamma globulin from it. Therefore, is must be kept sanitary.

The reason it has to be static free is because of a then-recent federal rule that required all plastic within the operating room to be anti-stat because of the use of oxygen in the operating room. My client needed the product fast.

I asked for a sample of an existing placenta pack and received it. I did some research and found that black anti-stat polystyrene was available and could be used in the product. I made a mold from the existing product and had a new anti-stat product made for my client.

It was my first job, and I was able to deliver the product within a week. I also set it up so that the client could manufacture the product. Thus, began a 30-year relationship with my first client.

How Can an Inventor Market a New Product?

Many students and others ask, "How does one market an invention?"

The answer essentially is that one just does not develop a new product for oneself, to satisfy one's genius. You don't invent, then sell the invention. One must step back from the work of inventing and look at what is needed, and by whom. An example can be drawn from the following experience with one of the large consumer companies in the midwest.

One morning my associates and I were having a "Creative Session," sitting around the large table in our conference room. One of our associates came in and put a product on the table. It was a new air freshener. It was the very first day that it appeared on the store shelves. Our colleague pointed out that this product was certainly going to be successful—and was going to take the place of the current big seller.

It was a wonderful product, made of thermoformed plastic with a gel in it and, like the competitive product, was designed to stand up on the toilet in the bathroom. It was much superior to the competitor in that, unlike the competitor, it didn't require its own box. It didn't require a screw top—it was just an attractive package that could hold about 1/8 lb. of gel.

The folks around the table "oohed" and "aahed" about the technical beauty of the product and how spectacular it was as a replacement.

Suddenly, the thought occurred to me that what we should do was aim a product at this new product—in other words, take the place of this new product with a superior product.

So, we sat around trying to figure out what kind of alternative would be superior. We talked about the gel as being similar. We talked about the package being thermoformed. We talked about all the various characteristics, and then one person said, "Why don't we make it turn itself on and off automatically, so that it would save itself for when it was really needed?" This was a new idea, but the question that arose immediately was, "How do we accomplish this?"

Several days later, I had occasion to go to a child's birthday party, and the answer came in a rush. When the birthday cake was brought out with all the candles lit, I walked past the cake and, lo and behold, the candles wavered in the wind.

That was the answer. We could make it turn itself on and off automatically by the use of the air in the room. The next question was, "How does one do that?"

As an aircraft pilot, I was aware of the Venturi System, which allows airplanes to fly and makes the propellers work. As a sailor, I knew the Venturi System was what made sailboats sail, even against the wind.

So, we essentially built a Venturi to capture the air and force it down through the throat and speed the air up, causing the fragrance of the gel to be forced out into the room.

When no wind was in the bathroom, no gel evaporated. When the wind was there because a person was there, the gel evaporated because there was wind. We had solved the problem, and we had a model. We subsequently built a 12′ × 14′ chamber and mounted a model of the air fragrance at one end and an electric fan at the other.

Now we wanted to make our model functional, so what could we do? We bought calcium tetrachloride at a chemistry house, put a little in the reservoir of the air freshener and introduced moist air into the fan. When the fan was turned on, it blew into the air freshener, and turned the air a smoky white. We knew that the air freshener was mixing the gel in the air. It was time to apply for a patent. (See Figure 6.)

We were then ready for a major presentation. I looked at the label of the product we were replacing and it had an 800 number listed. I called and asked the operator "Who's in charge of the new air freshener?" She said it was the Marketing Division, and the Marketing Division further directed me to the product manager. When I had the product manager on the phone, I said, "This is Stan Mason in Weston, Connecticut. I have a patent applied for on an air freshener which will take the place of your new product because it turns itself on and off automatically, without any moving parts." The product manager understood immediately how important such a product might be. He said, "How can I see this invention?" "Please visit us in Weston, Connecticut," I replied and gave him direction up the Merritt Parkway to our office. We set an appointment.

The next day we were cleaning up the office, and I was sitting looking through a book. The book had a quotation from Theodore Roosevelt:

> *Far better it is to dare mighty things, to win glorious triumphs, even though checkered by failure, than to take rank with those poor spirits who neither enjoy much, nor suffer much because they live in the grey twilight that knows not victory or defeat.*
>
> –Theodore Roosevelt

My mind leaped ahead, and I thought, supposing he says "no." So I asked one of our folks to go downtown and make an enlarged copy of the quotation and have it framed, then nail it up over the exit stairway.

The product manager visited us and was enthusiastic about the way the prototype worked. When the time came to leave–I knew that he had to go back and get permission to spend the money–he went down the stairs, looked up at the quotation, read it, then turned around and said, "I'll sign the agreement."

I had an agreement that he would take an option on the invention because I knew he couldn't take the large step of buying the patent directly. The option allowed him six months to study the product using the best science they had. The option was for $3,500 per month, for six months. If the client could not agree to take the license within that time, they could have an extension of another six months, for $5,000 per month, which actually was purchased by the client.

This sequence illustrates the importance of knowing how to organize, whom to attack, how to go about developing a product, and how to get an agreement.

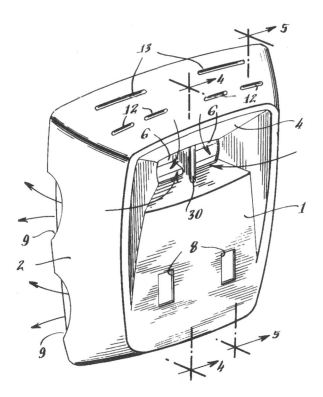

Figure 6. Air freshener

Making a Product
Better by Asking the Users

Simco, a company I founded in 1973 to foster inventive genius, was hired by a major bandage company to improve their standard product. They had a brilliant product manager who had a suspicion that the public preferred their product because it had the company's name printed on it, not because it was superior.

The product manager had competitive bandages made without the company name.

Focus groups were run, and these people indicated that the product manager was correct—the majority preferred the competitive bandage when names were not known. He hired Simco to created a new bandage that was truly superior to the competitive products.

Simco was going to have a difficult time because the client had just recently built new machines and any new product would have to be manufactured on these machines. Fortunately, I had been a machine designer while a senior in college and understood machines, speeds and feeds. The other criterion was that the new product would need to be made using a new kind of tissue paper that was 18 percent less expensive.

Simco designed 112 different versions of bandages, all of which could be made on existing machinery, using the lowest cost material. Ten of the 112 bandages were selected by the client with the help of focus groups. Simco then made these 10 into functional bandages and tried them with focus groups. Two were selected by the client as being appropriate in cost, and they were also easier to open than the old type.

The client modified one of the machines to make one of these bandages and introduced the new product. They then modified a number of the machines to produce the new bandage.

The company held the second bandage for later introduction, and five years later introduced the second type.

I think it's significant that our customer never told the consumer it was a new product. They simply made the advertising and the package say the bandage was better (and it was).

How Do You Change and Improve a Product?

Gelatin

Get others working on the project who know. One day while presenting findings to one of the big tea companies in their "serendipity room," the company president said, "Stan Mason, maybe you could help us with our gelatin problem." The problem was that gelatin sales were far off target. The reason was, according to the president, "Everyone has the gelatin in their kitchen cabinet, but no one is using it, probably because they're using Jello for dessert." The vice president of marketing said, "My wife says you can use this gelatin as a fertilizer for plants." Everyone laughed and slapped their thighs—everyone except the president and Stan Mason. I said, "You know, gelatin is essentially all protein, and it might well make a good fertilizer." The president said, "Why don't you organize a project and test this out?"

Simco had been working with a Ph.D. chemist in Texas on a horticultural project. With a specialty in plant physiology, he was the ideal person. He came to Simco, and we laid out a project. First of all, we wanted to find out what kind of plants were the most popular household plants. We called a research organization, and in two days they gave us the list of flowering and nonflowering plants popular in the household environment. There were 300 listed, and 30 were selected from the top of the list by Simco. We found that the University in Houston was enthusiastic about working with us. We also found that a 20′ × 40′ greenhouse could be built on the top of the science building in Houston for $20,000. The University would do the work if we could get the $20,000. It was an easy sell to the University because they really wanted to expand their program and didn't have the money in the budget for the greenhouse. The greenhouse was built in three weeks, and the program began. Our Ph.D. laid out a method of testing which included methods of applying the gelatin, and methods for measuring the differences between no gelatin and various quantities of gelatin. A standard potting soil was used, to which various solutions were added. An organized system of watering was developed, the plants arrived from all parts of the United States, and the large-scale investigation began.

It turned out to be a spectacular discovery in that, number one, you couldn't put too much gelatin on the plants—they would absorb it all. And, a small amount in a water solution on a weekly basis doubled the size of the plants in six weeks. We had an extremely efficient fertilizer available in almost every kitchen.

We hired a radio announcer who was a famous plant enthusiast. Every day, on his show, he would tell about this great discovery. He also wrote very persuasive copy for the label of the gelatin box.

The program went on for six months, and all the results were tabulated and publicized. The sale of gelatin suddenly increased, doubling its former volume to the point where it was necessary to build another factory to support the sales.

Figure 7. Gelatin fertilizer—new use for an old product

Anti-Spot

We worked for the sole manufacturer and marketer of a product used to prevent spotting in a dishwasher. They had many complaints from their customers saying that although the product worked very well, it got used up so fast as to be almost too expensive to use. They hired Simco to determine how to make the product last longer.

Simco studied the problem thoroughly and found that the device used in the dishwasher allowed far too much of the anti-spot product at first, and then subsequently far too little to be dispensed. The reason was that as water flowed through the anti-spot device too much would mix with the water. Then, as the amount of anti-spot declined, too little would mix with the water. Simco had to design a unique, controlled-release system. This was a very complex problem in that it had to be totally automatic as water filled the dishwasher.

Simco developed a system that automatically allowed a given amount of water to dilute a given amount of the anti-spot. With this metering system, the anti-spot material lasted twice as long and thus went twice as far.

The client was extremely happy with the new metering system, which was patentable.

Improving Premoistened Baby Wipes

This product is designed to clean a baby after the diaper has been removed. It is a super product and is sold very efficiently.

However, the product had a special problem in that when someone bought a package that had been on the store shelf for a long time, the moisture in the package migrated toward the bottom of the plastic box, leaving the wipes at the top dry to the touch. So, the product would not perform with anywhere near the efficiency that it would when fresh.

Simco studied the problem and determined that stacking paper in the box and then allowing a given amount of liquid to be deposited on the top of the stack was creating the problem. Simco developed a better way to package the product. Wrap each individual wipe around a roll, but independently. When a sheet was taken from the roll, it would rotate the whole roll about 1/2 of the circumference. This way, a different section of the roll would be on the bottom, and the moisture would be evenly distributed.

This solution was experimentally very successful, and the decision was made to purchase the new production equipment needed and introduce the product.

Dual Dispense Bottle

The client's conventional packages of cleaning fluid and window washing material were being sold to the public with only 15 or 20 percent solids. The rest was water.

The marketing division felt that if it were feasible to create a two-part package with concentrated liquid in one and an adjoining spray bottle to be filled with water by the consumer, the client would benefit greatly. Simco developed a special valve which could be put into the spray container's nozzle system that would combine the concentrate with the water in a ratio of 9 to 1 (the percentage the product required).

Simco presented many sequentially improved products until it was finally decided that the Simco system was patentable. Simco produced many plastic bottles of the new design. The water package and the cartridge package snapped together, and the design could easily accommodate a new concentrate package, replacing only the cartridge.

V.

INVENTIONS OF NEW PRODUCTS

T HE FOLLOWING EXAMPLES ILLUSTRATE three rules used by successful inventors:

- Identify and appraise opportunities for a new product or service
- Invent and develop a new product that can be commercially successful
- Market the invention

How to Learn about a New Product Area

Simco was engaged to help a company with new products in the dental field and felt that it was important to learn as much as possible about how dentists work.

Simco organized a series of dentist focus groups in California, Florida, Illinois and Boston. There were two types of dentists: dentists who were single practitioners, and dentists affiliated with a group.

Simco mainly learned that in California and Florida dentistry was much more advanced than in Illinois and Boston, and that while Boston dentists made beautiful porcelain teeth at $900 each, Florida dentists used a new kind of plastic at $50 a tooth. It was clear that a composite product was going to make new dentistry possible to the country.

Simco reported this study, and our client moved ahead to develop composites. It was found both appropriate and advantageous to get out of the business of making porcelains.

Experimentation–Inventing New Products for New Technology

In the early days of microwave ovens, I was very curious as to how they worked. They depended upon a magnitron which was the same unit that radar depended upon, and I was curious about radar. Having been a pilot, I learned that radar allows you to see through the clouds or fly at night in the dark.

I bought, via mail, a microwave unit. When it arrived, I opened the box and found a cookbook inside. The directions for cooking a chicken were as follows: Place a large glass dish in the microwave and put two saucers upside down on the dish. Then lay the chicken on the two saucers and cook for a few minutes. This was so intriguing to me that I immediately began the experiments.

Well, the experiment was a failure because the fat of the chicken got all over the plate, inside the oven and on the floor. I remember remarking this was a terrible way to cook a chicken.

At that point all of the marketing research on microwave units indicated that by 1985 fully 50 percent of U.S. kitchens would have a microwave. I realized that if this turned out to be true, none of the people with the microwave units would have had any microwave utensils at all. Further, they would have all kinds of problems evening out the energy produced by the oven. I determined to enter the microwave utensil business and create a group of microwave products to sell to companies in the cookware business.

Figure 8. Study new technology

One of the very first things that I needed to know was the pattern of energy distributed in a microwave oven so I could design the cookware to keep the food at the optimum spot. There were several pieces of technical equipment that could do this, but they were all very expensive. I determined a simpler way.

I laid out rows of popcorn on a plastic tray, put the tray in the microwave and turned the oven on. Where the energy was focused, the popcorn would pop; and where it didn't focus, the popcorn would not pop. I then raised the plastic tray, put more popcorn on, and eventually had a profile of where the energy was.

I designed microwave cookware to match the focus of the energy. In general, all the microwave utensils were oval or round and were raised up from the floor of the microwave by about one inch. Thus, energy coming into the oven from the magnitron would go in all directions, and would bounce from the bottom of the cavity through the food, cooking the food on the way down and the way back.

It was a very efficient system. We made prototypes out of clay and plastic and tested them in the microwave. Eventually we had an assortment of about 20 different units for various kinds of food. In estimating the types of foods that would most likely be cooked, it was important to realize that the family unit in the U.S. was becoming smaller, and many more women were working. I realized that families of the future would not rush home and cook a large turkey or great amounts of food. I designed the utensils for small families, and we began to develop recipes for the microwave.

Later I was in the first microwave store in Anaheim, California, with my son, and we were talking about our cookware. The store was empty except for one man who must have heard us speaking. He came over and asked, "Did I hear the word microwave utensils?" We said that this was true. "If you have microwave utensils and they work, you should visit us at the new microwave factory in Whittier. We're just opening it up and going into business," said the customer. My son and I drove 30 miles to Whittier and visited their home economist. She was most enthusiastic when she learned we had microwave cookware. She had never heard those words before. She questioned, "Does it work?" We demonstrated it to her in her kitchen. I had a unit which would cook both bacon and eggs simultaneously—and it could be eaten from. She brought over her boss to see the demonstration, and he then invited his boss, the president, who saw the advantages instantly. They ordered many thousands of dollars worth of microwave utensils to put in their microwave ovens, giving them a new product with which to demonstrate their microwave ovens.

The big problem was that we had only the prototype in our hand, yet we took a large order from the president, thanked him and then left. The question was how to get these made. The president had asked, "How much are they?" and I had estimated they would retail for $25.00 each. He had ordered 25,000 units.

My son and I left with a mission of finding some place in the U.S. where microwave cookware could be made inexpensively. We listed the needs we had for the utensils: They should withstand microwave energy, not absorb water, be attractive yet tough. We then learned of a company in Texas that had been making urinals but was going bankrupt because public building construction was down.

We visited this company and made an agreement with the owner to manufacture "Masonware," the name of the product. We ultimately had factories in Pennsylvania and California to produce 12 shapes that we marketed. We knew we had a unique new product matching the needs of the many brands of microwaves being produced. We launched a large-scale public relations campaign and sent photos and stories out to newspapers. We began demonstrations everywhere, and hired demonstration cooks to make presentations in large stores.

It was very successful. In two years, the category of "microwave cookware" totalled $350,000. Masonware flourished and became national, selling to Sears, Penneys, Bloomingdale's and thousands of smaller companies.

How Do You Make an Old Product New?

Disposable Diapers

During World War II, I was a flying instructor in Alabama teaching aviation cadets how to fly. My wife was with me, and we had our first son during this time. One afternoon as I stood in front of the table with my nude son facing up, my wife asked me to please put a diaper on the baby.

I picked up the diaper which was a square piece of cloth—and realized the diaper was square, and my son was round. Placing the diaper on him with giant safety pins was a real task, and my wife's instruction on the proper way to diaper a baby revealed how complicated it was.

Many years later, I was VP of Product Development for a major paper company, and one of my roles was to determine what future products would be. I went on a detailed search of supermarkets and drug stores and found a disposable diaper. It was square and made in Sweden— the very first that I had seen. Obviously, a square disposable diaper was not unique, and making them probably not a good business opportunity.

My company made paper towels, paper napkins, toilet paper, and many other disposable products. A disposable diaper might well fit into the mix to be sold through supermarkets to the consumers.

I set a project goal to make a disposable diaper without waste. After many experiments, all I needed to do was to take a pair of scissors and cut an origami-like pattern that folded up into a shape that fit the baby. It was held together by a sticky tape. I developed the product and established a patent for it. It was the first disposable diaper that fit the baby and was held on with sticky tabs.

The chairman of the company called me to his office and pointed out that I had wasted considerable money in the building of prototype machines because no one would use these diapers in place of cloth diapers. Later, the president sold the patent to another company whose farsighted chairman saw the opportunity. Other companies also went into the business using the same general concept.

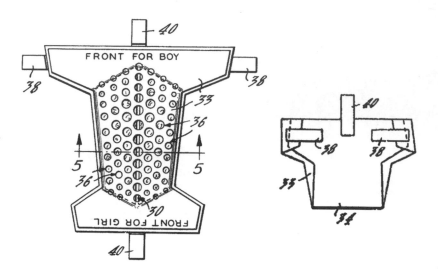

Figure 9. Disposable diaper

A Cosmetic Product

A certain cosmetic product, sold in tubes, was doing very well, but the product manager at a giant cosmetic company felt that perhaps their product could be adapted to compete with a similar product on pads, which were very effective for teenage pimples.

I called in to speak with the client, and we discussed how a new product in pads could be different and better than the existing competitor's product.

We finally determined that the best approach would be to make the pads themselves different and better than the competitor.

I had had some experience in nonwoven materials and thought that maybe we could make one side of the pad smooth and the other side rough—the first difference. The second difference would be that the pads themselves could be oval rather than round. The ovalness allows two uses of each pad. One side would be used first, and the other side second; whereas a circular pad can be grasped anywhere, an oval has a definite end. We checked these concepts with focus groups, and consumers found them useful and practical.

Thus we developed a new product, using existing chemistry and the same general packaging, but with the added difference of two useful sides. The product was established, manufactured and marketed in only four months.

Sanitary Napkins

A major sanitary napkin product was based on very good science and made by a leader in this field. Since I had the patent on the disposable diaper, and had worked for the company on many diaper improvements, I was asked if I could help them develop a superior sanitary napkin.

The big problem appeared to be leakage. One could see how the stains would be on the left and right side of the sanitary napkin. I called in my daughter, who is a marketing researcher, and asked her to get some plasticene at the art store. She then, at my request, met with an artist to copy some conventional, rectangular sanitary napkins out of clay. My daughter and the artist next wore these clay sanitary napkins, on nonmenstrual days, and we examined them after four hours of wear.

My goal was to determine the proper shape that would fit a woman precisely. (The shape of an hourglass developed from these experiments.) The artist tore apart rectangular sanitary napkins and cut and sewed them in the new shape. I then asked these young women to wear the sanitary napkins on menstrual days, which they did. The discovery was that this new shape did not leak.

We made many more and delivered them to the client. They became the standard product on the market.

How to Develop a New Product and Sell It

Always know your buyer and the means of production and distribution. When I was in California I was very interested in the garden supply stores. One company was the leader in California and was expanding its sales into nearby states. I studied some of their stores and tried very hard to discover a product that they didn't have but which could be sold very easily.

This company had six-sided redwood planters which they sold in high volume. These planters were all assembled and would nest, but would not fold up. The buyer had to take them home fully assembled and bulky. I thought that perhaps if I could design a rectangular planter box that would fold up and could be carried home under the arm there could be a real market for it.

I determined the dimensions of the ideal large flower box (18″ × 36″) and made drawings and a model. It was quite unique in that it required no nails to hold it together, and its bottom was not made of wood. It was a plastic tray. The plastic tray would hold all of the parts in a flat mode, which then could be subsequently set up and locked together at the corners with slide-on metal angles. I had the bottom vacuum formed and the sides and ends cut and held together with a 45-degree mitre. After I had finished the prototypes, I applied for a patent. (See Figure 10.)

I then telephoned the general manager of the company in California. I pointed out that I had a fold-up flower box that could be carried home and set up by the buyer, and the store could additionally sell the soil in plastic bags to fill it up. He was enthusiastic, and we arranged to meet.

It took about twenty seconds to set up the disassembled flower box, and the manager was impressed. He asked me how much it could be sold for. I wasn't sure, but I thought it would be around $39.00 and indicated that I would be happy with 7 1/2 percent of the wholesale price. He said "How about 6 percent?" and I said "Done." (I had already anticipated his cutting my price.)

The next month was spent setting up his factory, which was designed to make drawers for bedroom furniture and so was very inexpensive to set up. We designed a new label for the cover of the box, and we put six of the units in a corrugated container and had a beautiful label on the front. The company introduced it to all of their salespeople in one meeting.

The arrangement with the client was very satisfactory and created much income for Simco for 17 years, until

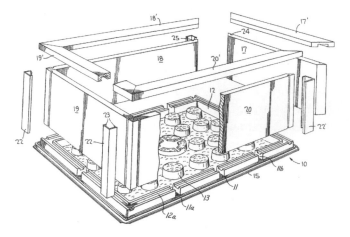

Figure 10. Fold-up flower box

the patent ran out. I subsequently sold the flower box to a competing company, and it sold very well even without patent protection.

How to Invent a
Product to Fill a Need

Surgical Mask

One of the big bandage companies called us at Simco and asked if we could make a full-face, disposable mask so that the doctor could wear glasses inside the mask.

We began by making a mask that would fit the average person's face and was held on with an elastic band. We visited NASA and talked with the surgeons who had worked on the masks for the astronauts. They had very interesting information. They told us that the face has very few nerves. They demonstrated this by taking two pencils with points about one inch apart and touching my face. I couldn't tell how many pencils were touching me until they were one inch apart. This gave us the clue as to how to make the mask. Because of the face's insensitivity, a loop could be fitted all around the face and be comfortable to wear. Thus we could provide the space to allow the doctor to wear glasses.

We designed the mask using the same material as in existing masks, but bent it in the center. It was a simple problem, but just hadn't been done before.

Fruit Bowl

My wife once asked me, "Can't you do something about the fruit spoiling in the fruit bowl?" Spoilage of fruit is a big problem in many homes and often more fruit is thrown away than is eaten. In thinking about the problem, I remembered a large warehouse in San Francisco filled with pears and peaches. Nitrogen was pumped into the warehouse to slow down the spoilage. Fruit in general gives off copious quantities of ethylene gas, encouraging fruit to spoil. The typical fruit bowl is circular and fruit, being the shape of a sphere, conforms to the inside of the bowl. Sugar from the fruit, the darkness and lack of air are ideal conditions for making fruit spoil. To reduce spoilage, all one needs to do is to raise the fruit from the surface of the inside of the bowl on ribs and support the fruit away from the bowl so that there's minimal surface contact.

I ran an experiment, and it proved very successful in reducing the spoilage. Further, I put holes in the bottom of the bowl, allowing air to circulate freely. I then engaged a potter to make a series of fruit bowls according to my drawings. The idea was to make the finished bowl of pottery, glass or plastic. The design was successful and patentable.

Sometimes a Problem Will Help Create a Product

My daughter was a freshman in college, and one morning she phoned me and said, "I'm really upset. Last night a scary thing happened to me." She lived in an old New England mansion which had been converted by the college administration into a large dormitory building. Each dormitory had four girls and one lavatory. The lavatory faced the front door of the apartment.

My daughter told me that she had gotten up in the middle of the night to use the bathroom. She went into the bathroom, but didn't close the door, so the inside of the front door was visible to her. She soon realized that someone outside was turning the knob of the front door, trying to get in. Fortunately the door was locked, but she was still very nervous about the experience.

A typical reaction of an inventor is to listen to such stories and then do some research to learn if there is an opportunity here.

I drove to the Westport, Connecticut, police station and talked with the Chief of Police. I repeated the story, and he told me that this was a typical modus operandi of a sneak thief–to try every door until one was found open. Then the thief would enter an apartment and quietly take whatever attracted him. Perhaps there was an opportunity here.

The solution to the problem would be a device telling the apartment owner that someone was trying to get in the front door. The device would have to be electronic, but could not be grounded or plugged into an electrical outlet because the door moves.

I called a friend who is an electronic genius. I described the problem to him, and we laid out a suggested electronic pattern and developed a bread-board which is hooked onto a doorknob. We designed the outside of the device, which looks something like the pattern illustrated in our patent (Figure 11). The product is currently being manufactured and sold.

Inventions Can Be New Methods

One day I was viewing the solar greenhouse between my library and the design workroom. It was laid out on an East-to-West course and received much light from the West. I wondered if I could determine a more efficient method for growing the Chinese Tallow Tree in relation to the sun (we were currently growing the trees in a hedgerow configuration so they could be harvested by machinery).

If trees are to be grown in the Earth's northern hemisphere, the row of trees should line up East to West so that any individual tree would receive sun in the morning and all day long, until the end of the day when the sun would be setting in the west. Think what an advantage if plants were oriented to receive the most sunlight all day long. Like solar receivers on the roof tops, plants would be oriented mainly to the south. They would receive maximum sun in the morning, noon and in the evening. They

Figure 11. Touch-responsive intrusion alarm

would receive much more sunlight than if, for example, they were planted in rows from north to south.

Then it occurred to me that corn, for example, would use much less water if it were planted in rows that were across prevailing wind, rather than in rows parallel with the prevailing wind. As an aircraft pilot, I know the main runways across the U.S. are WNW because that's the way the prevailing wind blows. Research shows that 20 percent less water would be used if the corn were planted across the prevailing wind, rather than with the prevailing wind.

Corn, as a plant, is very similar to the Chinese Tallow Trees, so I incorporated the use of water in the patent for my growth system, the abstract of which is shown in Figure 12. Because there were no U.S. patents in this field, and only one in France, and a few in Russia,

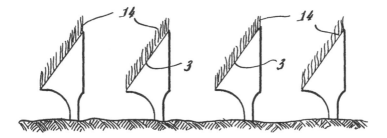

Figure 12. System for increasing growth of perennial crops

the patent was issued rather quickly as compared with other patents.

Interestingly, the day this patent was issued, the U.S. Navy released information that via satellite it was now able to locate ships—ours or others—anywhere in the world. I learned that this technology could also locate anywhere in the world a field of Chinese Tallow Trees or any other perennial hedgerow crop that is planted using this patented method, so that license fees can be collected from owners of that field.

Taking Risks: The Difference between Consultants and Employees

All of my experiences as an employee in different types of companies were truly wonderful experiences. In every case, I had extreme freedom and took advantage of that freedom to enhance my creativity. I realize now that no two employees work the same way or demonstrate the same kind of imagination or freedom of action. An example may be helpful.

When I was working at a large food company, I took one of the ads home and asked my wife if she could make one of the dishes. She reviewed the recipe and said, "I can't make this because if you put this much salt in it, it will taste awful." It took a person experienced in cooking to recognize whether the salt was too little or too much without cooking the dish. We did cook the dish, and it was terrible. I realized that the food company had no test kitchen, and we were depending on the advertising agency for any quality check.

That very day as I was walking around the office building, I saw a little house across the street, empty and for sale. I thought, "What a wonderful spot for a test kitchen. We could use the whole house, install extra stoves, and even do the photography for the ads right there in the living room. I believed the idea was great.

I was carried away and went to the real estate dealer and committed to buy the $20,000 house. My supervisor, a cautious person, assured me the owner would never approve such a purchase. So, I thought that the only way to get the money was to put it in my expense account. I slipped in $20,000 next to a $2.00 lunch and gasoline—and passed in my expense account. Naturally, the bookkeepers, who are good at checking numbers, bumped my expense report right up to the owner of the company, who wasted no time calling me in to his office.

When I explained that the $20,000 was for the testing facility necessary for a company of this size, the owner looked at me somewhat quizzically and said, "O.K., that's very good."

Figure 13. Buying a house on expense account

This is the kind of personality product developers need to develop. Otherwise, the risks that he or she proposes are too small and will not produce winning products.

It's always much easier to calm someone down and ask them to be less adventurous than it is to "light their fire." It's almost impossible to inspire someone to be more experimental or "risk taking."

We have worked with many companies, and in many cases, the product development people with whom we work have much trepidation and are generally nervous about making new products or ever presenting ideas to their bosses. We encourage them, with great enthusiasm, to take the risk. Of course, they are afraid they're going to be fired, but you can't make successful new things when you have a person with little imagination and/or little tolerance for risk.

PART III

SOME OF THE FUNDAMENTALS

VI.

ADDITIONAL THOUGHTS THAT
MAY BE HELPFUL TO YOU

HERE IS A LIST OF SOME ideas you may find helpful in your inventing work. Review them as a reminder.

You will need, at some point, to work with other professionals; they are, namely

Patent Attorney   Look for someone who is smart, experienced, and cooperative yet one who won't let you waste your time with less than potentially productive patents.

Lawyer   Find one who knows how to write short, uncomplicated agreements, someone who won't let you get into unproductive quarrels.

Accountant   This should be someone who knows what is best for you financially. A negotiator. One who knows the tax consequences of inventions and

royalties and how to help you
handle large funds.

If you are an inventor, you need these people right
now. Don't wait! And others in your life, too, are
important:

Your family   You need a partner who can
                               be independent and support-
                               ive of your endeavors.

Your friends   (You can't pick your family,
                               but you can pick your
                               friends.) They must not be
                               time wasters; you won't be
                               happy with spectator sports
                               buffs who spend hours dis-
                               cussing last Sunday's game.

Co-workers   Try to be around only those
                               who understand your pre-
                               occupations and support
                               your dreams.

Administrative Assistant   who remembers details
                               such as paying bills, your
                               appointments for weddings
                               and dinners. Most impor-
                               tant, they must find things
                               you lose.

Here are some principles to aid with your own
understanding of the finiteness of time:

1. Commit yourself to accomplishment. Mentally, look ahead a week, a month, a year. Mark the calendar as to what should happen, on what date, to achieve your goal.

2. Think big or you'll accomplish only small things.

3. Say good-bye to the eight-hour day of work. Get up early.

4. Say good-bye to weekends. They are an inventor's best time because everybody else is away doing their thing.

5. Learn concentration in the center of chaos. Ignore distractions that would demand your attention.

How to invent the right things? First, be a student of the continuum of life. Watch for signals of social and technological change. Where they "cross," there's a product vacuum. For instance, Masonware Corporation and its products came out of a study of social change—the increase of numbers of working women and, at the same time, microwave oven development. The need is to save time with a quick-cooking appliance—the microwave oven—and the need for new cooking utensils to use with this oven (pots and pans wouldn't work). Look for new technology replacing old.

Here are a few methods you can use to keep up on things and fire your enthusiasm:

1. Reading: What is the news?

2. Travel: What are they buying?

3. Talk with all kinds of people. What are they saying?

4. Visit factories. All kinds. See what the new processes are.

5. Work for other companies in diverse roles. Learn their new product needs and their new marketing strategies and tactics.

6. Use focus groups to forecast future wants and needs.

One of the most efficient and effective ways to benefit from your creativity and innovation is to license your invention to a company already in the general business category of your innovative product. (In effect, a license is similar to "renting" your patent or your know-how to someone else.)

The successful inventor, or innovator, invents not in an area of personal interest, but in the product category of a company already in a business—where a better or new product can easily be manufactured and then marketed.

Do not invent a product that you like. Rather, spend your creative energies developing a product or a service which you feel someone else likes; ideally, invent "for" a company already in the field, with manufacturing facilities capable of building your product and marketing skills and personnel able to take your product into the class of trade, the stores, or the supermarket shelf, where they already have products being sold.

Invent or innovate products for a customer, even though the customer may be the company that will license your product, manufacture it and sell it wholesale to the retail store where your ultimate consumer will shop. In fact, your customer may be the company you work for.

You must keep your eye on the ultimate purchaser of your product. He or she is your target. Consumers must see in your product or service an obvious benefit for which they will exchange money and feel that it is a worthwhile bargain.

Licensing Your Product

Assuming you have gone through these rigorous steps, have found a target for your inventive spirit and now have a specific item to make in a unique fashion, you are ready to consider the licensing process.

You are prepared for the license process if, in fact, you have a patent applied for, if you have a lawyer in the background to help you arrange the proposal and you have an accountant who has helped you determine future costs of bringing the products to market.

How does one get in contact with the prospective licensor of your invention? It's been my experience that very often the best way is the simplest way: Pick up the telephone and call the company. Speak to the operator and ask, "Who in Marketing is responsible for the widget business?" The operator will probably tell you, "I don't know. I'll let you speak to the Marketing secretary." And from the Marketing secretary, you will probably discover the person responsible for the widget business.

Your conversation with the Product Manager might well go: "Ms. Jones, I'm a Product Developer." (Never say "inventor" because this title gives you an aura of a wild-eyed dreamer. "Product Developer" is much more down to earth, business-like and believable.)

"Ms. Jones, I have developed a product I believe will make your current model, which I see on the shelves, obsolete. I have a patent applied for, a model built and cost estimates developed."

Ms. Jones certainly doesn't want to hear that her best selling product may be obsolete. She knows she must see you because her future depends on ferreting out future competition and finding new opportunities for herself and her company.

If your conversation is successful, she may ask where *you* are. Tell her your town name and invite her to visit you.

I have found that fully 50 percent of the time the Product Manager, Vice President or President, after discussion, will visit the product developer or at least meet in a hotel lobby in a city half-way between.

Meeting Your Prospect

Following is a basic checklist of what you need when you meet your prospect to sell your invention. First of all, make a written agenda, and keep to it.

1. **You need a patent (or patent applied for).** Serious people won't talk to you otherwise. They might ask you to sign a nondisclosure

agreement. Talk to your patent attorney, but the chances are it won't hurt your case to sign the agreement.

2. **Don't go alone.** Someone needs to help observe what happens at the meeting. Someone needs to take detailed notes. Your attention will be on the sweep of talk, not on details. Someone needs to watch the other participants of the meeting to see what they find of particular interest or to make sure they don't spirit off a drawing without your knowledge.

3. **Speak to the top person.** She or he may be the Product Manager or someone else, but you will be looking for a decision maker. Don't be shy to ask if the listener to your story can say, "O.K., I'll buy."

4. **Have an idea of what you want from the meeting.** You want a deal of some kind. What do you want?

   • **Do you want to sell an option?** Do you want to sell an exclusive arrangement? An option might be: You want $10,000 (plus or minus) for, say six months, for your prospect to study your invention to see if it fits their product category, manufacturing facilities, marketing skills, experience, personnel and customer profile. Are you going to see only one prospect? If so, it can be an exclusive option. If you are going to present products to more than one prospect and let them bid, it must then be, of course, a nonexclusive option.

- **Royalties**—you need to know how much royalty you are looking for. And you need an assurance the company is actually going to produce the product if you license it to them.

  Royalties can range all over the map. In general, the higher the volume, the lower the retail price, the smaller the percentage of the wholesale costs. That is, if you sell a bolt, the royalty may be as low as a tiny percent of the wholesale price, but if you are selling a new kind of locomotive, where the individual price is high and volume is low, the royalty percentage of the wholesale price might be as high as 50 percent. Much also depends on the uniqueness, the value to the customer and the potential strength of the patent position.

  Lastly, you need permission to audit the financial books, so you will see that you are actually receiving royalties on the number of items actually manufactured and sold.

- **You might want a front-end payment.** This could be as high as $20,000, $30,000 or $40,000 against future royalties. Once the company pays this sum, they might as well go into production to get that front-end payment back.

5. **Have a good model, if possible.** The model should be close to your perception of the finished product and should be good enough to convince a customer that it's a real product. It should function if at all possible.

6. **You need posters and drawings.** A drawing done on blueprint paper or a computer printout could convince your prospective purchaser that you have actually gone through the engineering steps and computations.

7. **Try to understand the market for the invention** in terms of who needs the invention (customers of the prospect). You need to estimate the volume of the consumer needs. For instance, what is the possible number of units that can be sold in the first six months, second, third, etc. You want an estimate of dollar sales.

8. **You want an outline in writing of your research results** or other proof or indications of consumer or customer need. You need to interview potential prospects and write reports on what the prospects said.

9. **You need a careful estimate of tooling costs.** If your invention is a plastic product, for example, you need to go to people who know about tool-

ing and plastic production. What kind of material is best? What resources are needed?

10. **You must have a list of marketing plans.** How would you sell the product? With what kind of advertising? A slogan will explain the product's benefit in a few words. Remember the ad about the first Volkswagon? Its headlines were "Think Small" and a picture of the bug.

11. **Take your accountant with you** to do the negotiating.

12. **Don't take your lawyer.** More deals are broken by legal details than made.

13. **Sign their Confidentiality Statement** (if you have a patent pending). Otherwise, they might not look at your invention at all.

14. **Most important: Don't get bogged down with the technical details or the tricky science which you love.** All a company is interested in is how to make money—they are really not interested in your invention. Remember, the bottom line is how your invention will fill their pocketbook.

15. **Keep careful notes** of who said what to whom. Hold them to their word. Document everything.

16. **Don't let their lawyer hold up the agreement.**

17. **Try to get a "reasonable" rather than a grand front-end payment.** Let it be against future royalties, if necessary. Balance possible royalties

with high volume. If unit cost is low and volume is great, small royalties are O.K. If unit cost is high and volume is low, high royalties are expected.

18. **A repeat: Be sure you have legal power to get a look at their books** to see if they are paying enough royalty.

19. **Be sure any improvements they make to your invention are yours too,** so they won't "invent" you out of a royalty.

20. **Follow up relentlessly.** Begin writing letters 10 minutes after the meeting. Send copies to all who were at the meeting.

Don't Get Discouraged

At times, you might not get quite the reception you hoped for. If this happens, prepare to bolster your confidence and pursue your leads.

- They may call in their R&D Director who will say "they've been thinking about your idea over the years" or "they tried it and it won't work" or "the cost you estimated for production is too low."

- Their marketing person will say he doesn't believe it can be explained to consumers. The selling price you estimated is too high.

- They'll ask for your model and your posters for their study. They'll take it to their boss, or study it to death or perhaps duplicate it with some twist.

- They'll be enthusiastic about all aspects and will tell you you're a genius and that they'll get back to you. Maybe they will and maybe they won't.

You will have to choose how much energy to expend in following up or moving on to a new prospect.

VII.

LAST THOUGHTS

EVERYBODY HAS 24 HOURS per day. As an inventor, your goal is to produce more results per day than a noninventor. Why? Because you are your own overhead. Your brain is your best capital.

The easy way is to work harder. And longer. Use scraps of time. Carry pencil and paper. Keep a "laboratory" notebook, day by day. It will soon have a life of its own. It is valuable for other things too, like ownership of your ideas.

You will need travel time to sell ideas; Never cross the country to see only one prospect—line up a group. Use the cheap seats on the planes.

Make models and sketches. See if your idea really, really works.

Don't fall in love with another project before you've completed and started selling the present one.

Take pleasure in what you're doing. It can be exhilarating to solve that self-imposed problem. It is more satisfying than almost anything else. It is a hobby. But unlike other hobbies, it can make you rich.

Practice self-discipline. Don't work to the exclusion of all things, but don't wander around looking at your real estate. Work on things that matter.

Set goals for accomplishment.

Keep a calendar. Plan at least a month ahead.

Star important meetings.

Get up early.

Postpone administrative tasks: bill paying, fixing the car, and so on.

Communicate! Use the telephone. Use computer searches. Use your library. Talk to whomever can teach you what you need to know.

Practice secrecy. Don't get your kicks by telling everybody your ideas. It is counterproductive, and could be expensive. Months later, you could see your idea claimed as someone else's.

Don't invent too early or too late. At least don't try to market an invention too early or ahead of its time. Too late is costly, too.

Learn the value of mistakes. Mistakes teach. If you are not making mistakes, you aren't taking chances. Taking chances is what gets results. The greater the risk, usually the greater the payoff.

Learn to learn. Invest great effort in becoming a quick study. Learn to grasp unrelated data fast. Hone your memory. Teach yourself to grab the big picture quickly. Test yourself by repeating the information to yourself. Observe. Construct estimates in your mind of quantities, trends, past history. Remember numbers. Teach yourself to guess and estimate all kinds of things—RPM's, weight, speed, how many, how big, how does it work?

Recognize all aspects of the reality you live in. Build awareness of what lies behind and ahead of that reality. Question how things are today, and wish, imagine, conjure how it could be replaced by some method or thing which would be better, cheaper, simpler, tastier, lighter.

Do your homework, day in, day out. Read all the popular and technical publications you can which directly or remotely affect your field. Travel. Observe people and phenomena. Watch television. Know what your potential customers and consumers know. Experience the same things.

Lastly, aim for excellence, not perfection. Make your inventions, your innovations, your models, your charts, your computations *excellent*, not perfect. Excellence takes minutes or hours or days. Perfection may delay you forever.

Appendix: Creativity

The notes in this appendix are selected from my textbook titled Creativity. *This 214-page text is used in the courses I teach on innovation and entrepreneurship.*

These notes can be used for self-assessment and as cue-cards for actions to improve the reader's creativity. Review them, one by one. They represent some of what we know about creativity and creative people, and how creativity is applied to find, develop, and market successful new products.

A creative act is never an accident. Some appear accidental. But always there was a prepared mind that had previously been "wishing" for an accident that fills a gap or answers the unasked question.

Creativity is not inherited, nor does it come from the environment. It comes from inside a person. Everyone can be creative to some degree. There is ordinary creativity—departing a little from the usual ways by modifying old things and improving them. And there is special creativity that creates humanity's great achievements. Only a handful in each generation reach great creative heights. But many can enrich their lives with ordinary creativity.

We can define four steps in the creative process:

1. Preparation (collecting ideas)

2. Incubation (letting the mind think about the ideas)

3. Illumination (solution)

4. Verification (checking)

Poets, scientists and artists all experience these same general steps.

Applying the creative process, the successful inventor will typically include some additional steps:

1. Observing an opportunity; seeing a gap in satisfying a current or developing need

2. Studying all available information about the need and current products

3. Conceptualizing new and better ways to satisfy the need

4. Researching many possible solutions, including cost/value estimates

5. Searching for a creative resolution—something new, different

6. Aha! Finding an invention

7. Developing and testing the invention, proving out both manufacturing (cost) and marketability (value)

8. Successfully selling the invention

The eighth step is not part of the invention process, but is the purpose of the process, and the measure of its success.

However we describe the creative process, there are steps to go through to produce creative ideas. Sometimes the various steps of creative thinking are simultaneous.

In creativity, it is thinking that counts over memory. There are three characteristics of productive, creative thinking: flexibility, originality and fluency–the ability to produce lots of ideas at one sitting. And it's important to see the whole broken into its various parts and then seeing all again to create the new.

Questions are central in creative thinking. But desire is not enough–background helps. Immersion in the field and preoccupation with the problem is essential. Problems "get inside" the creative person . . . until the creative solution gets them out. Problems refuse to let the creative mind rest.

See things in a childlike way. Then apply adult logic. Controversy? Settle controversy through research, not argument.

Sometimes solutions in one area are valid in others. Look around.

Ponder the strange, the unusual, the striking, the new phenomena. Unusual events inspire thinking. Odd results pose questions that need investigation. Strange phenomena arouse wonder and creative questioning.

Look for identity among two or more things regarded as unrelated. Anyone could see an apple fall. Newton saw the law of gravity.

Negative results can point the way to new knowledge. After 600 tries in an experiment, Edison was chided at lack of success. He replied, "We know a lot. We know 600 ways which won't work."

In creative problem solving, begin by assessing the problem before labeling it. Use a system—a series of proven steps. Here's a five-step system:

1. Assess the situation. Ask questions. Ask them endlessly. Answers will suggest new questions.

Be intelligently ignorant. Gather facts relentlessly. But consider "facts" opinions, until rigorously tested. Search for the key factor. In almost every situation one particular fact will turn out to be more important than any other.

2. Define the problem. Write it out on paper and check it carefully to assure you have defined the real problem.

3. Use your subconscious. Let your mind do the work without pushing. Use your stored knowledge.

4. Produce ideas. Record them all. Brainstorming helps.

5. Select the best idea. Talk with others. The total experience of several people can apply expanded knowledge to find the best of several ideas.

Remember:

• A situation can be poorly assessed even when everyone is working hard on it.

• Invalid assessments can mislead disastrously.

• It's easy to accept opinion as fact.

• Poor assessments inspire erroneous conclusions.

• Emotion-inspired adjectives are insidiously misleading.

- "Facts" must be questioned until the questioning hurts.

- Check with personal observation.

- Be careful of anything you think of as a fact. Is it? Really? Challenge premises. And remember—a question can have more than one answer.

Time changes facts into semifacts or perhaps into nonfacts. Check judgments regularly to see if the "facts" are now different. Observe personally. Learn for yourself. It is tough, demanding. It produces grist from which one can build strong, new relationships in ideas. Read about it, but experience it first-hand if at all possible. I consider "hands on" indispensable.

What is thinking? To think is to exercise the powers of judgment, conception and inference—to reflect for the purpose of reaching a conclusion. Thinking is one of the great pleasures of life.

The creative mind is chided to think, to question the way things are now done.

Be ready to break habits, if you would be productively creative.

A checklist of questions can give us new points of view. But it is up to us to pursue each question to see where it can lead. Alex Osborn, a mentor of mine, provided me with this checklist of questions: Put to other uses? New way to use as is? Other uses if modified? Adapt? What else is like this? What other ideas does this suggest? Does past offer parallel? What could I copy? Whom could I emulate? Modify? New twist? Change meaning, color, motion, sound, odor, form, shape? Other changes? Magnify? What to add? Greater frequency? Stronger? Higher? Longer? Thicker? Extra value? Plus ingredient? Duplicate? Multiply? Exaggerate? Minify? What to subtract? Smaller? Condensed? Miniature? Lower? Shorter? Lighter? Omit? Streamline? Split up? Understate? Substitute? Who else instead? What else instead? Other ingredient? Other material? Other process? Other power? Other place? Other approach? Other tone of voice? Rearrange? Interchange components? Other pattern? Other layout? Other sequence? Transpose cause and effect? Change pace? Change schedule? Reverse? Transpose positive and negative? How about opposites? Turn it backward? Turn it upside down? Reverse roles? Change shoes? Turn tables? Turn other cheek? How about a blend, an alloy, an assortment, an ensemble? Combine units? Combine purposes? Combine appeals? Combine ideas?

To gain the most value from such a list, we first twist each question around until it applies to our problem. Then we carry the thought-train through on an exploratory journey to see what ideas result. Brainstorming is a useful method. It can be beneficial to make a checklist of questions specifically for your type of work.

In brainstorming, ridiculous ideas can be pearls of great value. Technology is so advanced today, even seemingly foolish ideas can lead to creative inventions.

Put yourself inside the problem. You might ask, "What does it feel like to be inside the lawnmower when the starter rope is pulled?" or other inside-the-problem-kind-of-question. Models from nature can be used to solve mechanical problems in products.

In the creative work of scientists, technologists, and business people, the flash of insight is revealed. In science it is revealed in the statement of the hypothesis; in the art of disciplined conversation, in the asking of the right question; in logic, in the drawing of the premise; in problem solving, in the recognition or statement of the problem.

Look at a lot of related things to set off the spark. Know as much as possible about the area you want to create within. Gobble up ideas, facts, concepts, details, generalities, dimensions, colors, etc. Tiny details, if observed, make a tough problem solvable. Discovery really is a function of being constantly on the alert, observing automatically, even while deep into something else. Discipline favors the flash of creative insight. One verifies an insight by trying out the idea.

The white heat of enthusiasm also helps fan the fires of creative invention. "Emotion moves us," say men and women of art and science. Passion is a source of creativity. One is not as much conscious of the ideas as possessed by them. Invention comes out of deep, passionate drive.

Rigid personalities don't make inventions.

These are conditions that favor discovery: quiet mind, preparation, ordered storage, observation, stimulation, quiet, time and patience.

To find a solution, look at the problem from a completely different point of view.

Thirst for knowledge is essential to the creative person. More than that, he or she must accumulate facts. What is already known about a subject area by others? By books? First, try the library. Study catalogs. Understand competitors' products, products that have basic similarities but are for different purposes. Stretch the analogies! Find out what associates think about the problem. Talk with everyone about the subject. Read, read, read. Imagination thrives on knowledge. Study fundamental principles and laws. Ask associates to study separate sources of information, then summarize together.

Watch out for words like "only," "always," and "never." Even in your own mind they are deterrents.

What "everybody knows to be true" probably isn't.

Don't be too hard on a new idea. It is just a baby and might be a "correct answer" when it is developed a bit further.

Later knowledge makes eminently practical that which was thought impossible at an earlier time.

It is difficult or perhaps impossible to solve a problem without understanding the underlying principles.

Simple solutions are often best.

FURTHER READING

Baldwin, J., *BuckyWorks*. John Wiley, 1996.

Rossman, Joseph, *Industrial Creativity*. University Books, 1964.

Franklin, Reece A., *Inventor's Marketing Handbook: A Complete Guide to Selling and Promoting Your Invention*. AAJA Publishing Co., 1989.

DeBono, Edward, *Eureka! An Illustrated History of Inventions from the Wheel to the Computer*. Rinehart and Winston, 1974.

Clark, Ronald William, *The Scientific Breakthrough: The Impact of Modern Invention*. Putnam, 1974.

MacCracken, Calvin., *A Handbook for Inventors: How to Protect, Patent, Finance, Develop, Manufacture, and Market Your Ideas*. Scribner, 1983.

Tripp, Alan R., *Millions from the Mind: How to Turn Inventions (Yours or Someone Else's) into Fortunes*. Amacom, 1992.

ABOUT THE AUTHOR

Stanley I. Mason is an internationally known inventor and entrepreneur. He has created and patented many well-known products, including the first shaped disposable diaper, unique Band-Aids, the first granola bars, the first microwave cookware, new sanitary napkins and tampons, cosmetics and hair care products, paper towels and tissues, snack food, hamburger and pizza packaging, fingerprint printing systems, and many toys, games and talking dolls.

He has established four entrepreneurial companies and served as visiting entrepreneurial specialist with Johnson Wax, Hoechst-Celanese, and others. He is Director of Entrepreneurship at the University of Connecticut School of Business and teaches Entrepreneurship in the MBA program. Mr. Mason has lectured at more than 20 colleges and universities in the United States, Canada and Hawaii and is a key speaker at conferences and symposiums on innovation and entrepreneurship. He founded the Mason Research Foundation to investigate the technical and economic feasibility of the Chinese Tallow Tree as a plantation-scale crop for fats, oil and fuel. The Foundation also organizes and leads faculties in China, Russia and the Congo teaching entrepreneurship, free enterprise and invention. Earlier in his career Mr. Mason held executive positions at Hunt Foods, Martin Aircraft, Armstrong, American Can and U.S. Steel.

He was a fighter pilot in World War II. In 1973 he founded Simco to foster inventive genius. Simco has created more than 100 new products for more than 40 Fortune 500 companies. Simco has a task force of 125 specialists around the nation who serve as product consultants to major corporations.

Mr. Stanley I. Mason, Jr., President and CEO, Simco, Inc., 61 River Road, Weston, CT 06883